A Day in
Quarantine
with Jordyn

Jordyn's Journeys

By Tracey Smith

Archway Publishing books may be ordered through booksellers or by contacting:

Archway Publishing
1663 Liberty Drive
Bloomington, IN 47403
www.archwaypublishing.com
844-669-3957

ISBN: 978-1-6657-1595-9 (sc)
ISBN: 978-1-6657-1596-6 (hc)
ISBN: 978-1-6657-1597-3 (e)

Print information available on the last page.

Archway Publishing rev. date: 01/05/2021

Dedication

This book is dedicated to my daughter
and my grand-daughter.

Mommy, what are we doing
today? I'm so bored.
Can we bake, make and taste today?

I like when we bake cookies or cupcakes, and I love putting icing on them and decorating them with sprinkles.

I like when we make forts
inside for us to play in.

I like hanging out inside the forts, and
I love when we read books together.

I like when we make new juices to taste and mix them up in the juicer!

Some of them I like and some of them I don't like.

Can we make one with mango today? I love mango Mommy!

Can we play inside or outside today?

I love when we play outside, and I ride my scooter or go for a walk in the park with you.

Mommy, I like when we sleep in
and watch a movie together.

Can we do a Zoom call with my friends from school today too, so we can talk and see each other? Can I do some art and paint a picture with my friends on Zoom? I really miss seeing my friends and playing with them. Please say yes Mommy!

Yes, Jordyn. We can bake, and we can make stuff today! We can taste juices today too! Are you ready for a green machine juice? It's so good for you!

Jordyn, we can also play inside and outside today! I love our walks and talks together when we are outside getting some fresh air and walking the dog.

And yes, we are going to call your friends on Zoom today too, and do some artwork! I know they miss seeing you. I know it's hard not being able to see your friends face-to- face, and not being able to give them hugs, or to get hugs back from them. So are you ready to get started Jordyn? Yes, Mommy, I'm ready!

We can watch a movie and play in a fort together. Let's bake some cupcakes and taste some juices today too!

Mommy, we did a lot today. What a busy day I had, and now I'm getting tired.

Before I go to bed and we read a book together, can we Facetime Ma-Ma and Pop-Pop? I want to tell them about everything I did today!

I know they can't wait to hear all about it. Ma-Ma and Pop-Pop love Facetiming with me.

Of course you can Jordyn, and I'm so glad you are not bored anymore!

Printed in the United States
by Baker & Taylor Publisher Services